New Christian (

Smile, Pl

Collected by

Phil Mason

MONARCH
BOOKS

Mill Hill, London NW7 3SA and Grand Rapids, Michigan 49501

Copyright © Phil and Mary Mason 2001.
The right of Phil and Mary Mason to be identified as authors of this work has been asserted by them in
accordance with the Copyright, Designs and Patents Act 1988.

Published by Monarch Books 2001,
Concorde House, Grenville Place, Mill Hill, London NW7 3SA.

Distributed by:
UK: STL, PO Box 300, Kingstown Broadway, Carlisle, Cumbria CA3 0QS;
USA: Kregel Publications, PO Box 2607, Grand Rapids, Michigan 49501.

ISBN 1 85424 558 9 (UK)
ISBN 0 8254 6036 0 (USA)

British Library Cataloguing Data
A catalogue record for this book is available from the British Library.

Cartoons by Mike Buecheler

Designed and produced for the publishers by
Gazelle Creative Productions
Concorde House, Grenville Place, Mill Hill, London NW7 3SA.
Printed in Singapore.

Two members of the Mormons knocked on the door and engaged the householder in conversation. They then asked if she would benefit from learning about Jesus.

"No," she answered confidently, "We are members of the United Reformed Church."

It was a very hot summer's day, but beautifully cool inside Winchester Cathedral. An American visitor came up to me and in all seriousness commented, "I really must congratulate you on the air conditioning in here."

"That's nothing," I replied, "You should try it in winter."

Another visitor asked: "Gee, how did they heat this place in Roman times?"

Another queried: "Do they hold services here?"

Winchester Cathedral is cleaned by a willing band of helpers, affectionately known as the Holy Dusters. One day a visitor from another cathedral enquired, "Who cleans all the brass?"

"The Holy Dusters," came the reply. There was a pause.

"Ah," the visitor said rather awkwardly, "We just use ordinary ones."

Our local radio station has a very popular Sunday breakfast programme. One morning the presenter said,

"I had better give you the correct time now, in case you need to get to church, or to go somewhere important."

A Salvation Army captain was collecting at a local service station.

"I am sorry," said a sad-looking middle-aged lady. "I can't give you anything, I've just lost my husband."

Full of love and Christian compassion, the captain asked, "And how long ago since you lost him?"

With a quick look round she replied, "Well, about five minutes ago. I think he must have gone to the toilets."

I was attending my grandmother's funeral in London, with all the family assembled.

We stood for the first hymn, and my uncle looked down to see blood running along the back of the pew. In dismay he put his arm around my aunt, fearing the worst: after all, we were at a funeral. She looked around, gasped — and felt in her pocket.

The top had come off her cough medicine.

The choir at the local Methodist church wore blue serge gowns, which on top of their ordinary clothes could make them feel very hot at times. One warm Sunday the ladies decided to take off their dresses before donning their gowns.

When the preacher stood up, he removed his gown because of the heat — and invited the choir to do the same.

While decorating the church hall our minister fell off a ladder and broke his ankle. His wife, a lay preacher, volunteered to take the service the following Sunday. We warned her that she must avoid a hymn which he had taught us a few weeks before: "We Are Climbing Jacob's Ladder". She took great care in choosing the hymns, and felt quite safe with "I Will Sing the Wondrous Story".

Safe, that is, until we reached verse three and found ourselves singing, "Bruised was I from many a fall".

Hospitality

A definition from Archbishop Donald Coggan:
"Real hospitality is the art of making people feel
at home — when you wish they *were* at home."

The sidesman was taking the collection at a fashionable London church. He waited patiently while the visitor fumbled in his pockets. At last the visitor sighed and gave up, muttering, "I can't find any small change."

"That's quite all right, sir," replied the sidesman. "It isn't small change that we want."

A baptism was being held during the main Sunday morning service at a central London church well known for its ritual and ceremony. The family had reserved seats for the occasion.

As Grandad, not a dedicated

churchgoer, made his way down the aisle he spotted the picket stand with its array of lighted candles. Admiring the blaze, he exclaimed, "I didn't know we were having a barbeque!"

The wife of the major at the Salvation Army Citadel was responsible for the children's slot in the morning service at Christmas. She indicated that with the help of a number of children she was going to display an acrostic on a well-known Christmas word.

They practised in the hall upstairs and then came confidently trooping onto the platform, facing the congregation, but in reverse order. The word should have been STAR.

As a soldier in The Salvation Army I used to accompany the Commanding Officer to sell the *War Cry* in local pubs. No matter what rank the officer held, one landlord always referred to him as 'lieutenant'.

One Friday evening the landlord made his customary greeting, to which our C.O. replied, "I'm a captain now, I have two pips on my shoulder, not one." Hearing this, one of the locals leaning on the bar commented, "The more pips, the bigger the lemon."

We made good sales that night.

Recipe for a happy marriage:

The wife should love her husband a little and understand him a lot.

The husband should love his wife a lot, and never try to understand her at all.

The local Salvation Army corps at Elgin in north Scotland, though quite small, managed to attract large numbers for special events. One Christmas the captain had written an Advent play making liberal use of both spotlights and music. There was, however, only one electric socket, which meant that considerable dexterity was required to effect changes.

Towards the end of the play, following the angel's announcement, the captain experienced a problem removing the plug for the spotlight. An extra tug resulted in the plug coming suddenly free, and a surprised captain fell through the curtains, landing at the feet of a row of elderly ladies. From the row behind a voice sang out, "Lo, he comes with clouds descending…"

An elderly retired vicar, a friend of the bride's parents, was asked to officiate at a wedding in a parish church in the north of England. While the couple were kneeling on the chancel steps following their exchange of vows, the old man whispered that during the next hymn they should follow him to the altar for prayers.

He announced the hymn, turned, and paced slowly towards the altar.

To the amusement of the choirboys, the couple followed, much entangled in the bride's dress. And still on their knees.

When my husband and I became engaged, I had no one to give me away at the wedding. Being very close to our rector, I asked him to do the honours. Father D. had been a missionary in the Philippines and he told Dan, my fiancé, that it was customary for the groom to present the father of the bride — or in this case, the rector himself — with a rice field and five water buffalo.

Father D. went on to explain that he would be willing to forego the rice field, this being hard to come by in New York City. However, he could not sanction the marriage without the buffalo.

This became a parish joke. At our wedding rehearsal Dan was startled by the cry from those around: "Dan, where are your water buffalo?"

I was taking the wedding for a vicar who was indisposed. The verger handed me a list of hymns. Instead of 298 she had accidentally written 289, which I duly announced. So instead of singing, "Praise my soul the King of Heaven..." we launched with gusto (and to the consternation of the vicar's wife) into, "Soon will you and I be lying/Each within our narrow bed" — a selection from the funeral section of the hymnbook.

While reading banns of marriage recently I accidentally spoonerized the notice at the end, saying: "If anyone knows any just cause or impediment why these persons may not be joyfully loined together..."

From an Oxford church magazine:

"We apologise for a misprint which appeared in last month's issue referring to our fête opener, General Jamieson, as 'battle-scared'. It should of course have read 'bottle-scarred'."

A boat crashed onto the rocks and began to sink.

"Does anyone know how to pray?" shouted the skipper.

"Yes, I do," cried a zealous Christian, leaping to his feet.

"Good," said the skipper. "You pray, the rest of us will put on our life-jackets. We're one short."

"How would you tackle the drink problem?" a rather pious lady asked a priest of the Community of the Resurrection, Mirfield.

"With a corkscrew," he replied.

The rector of a church in Nottinghamshire was visiting an aged and ailing parishioner. She fixed him with a stern gaze. "When I die, rector," she insisted, "I want you to take my funeral. I can't hear that young curate at all."

Prayer for mornings:

Dear God,
So far today I'm doing all right. I have not gossiped, lost my temper, been greedy, grumpy, nasty, selfish or over-indulgent. However, I'm getting out of bed in a few minutes and I will need a lot more help after that.

A little boy asked his mother why the vicar got four weeks' holiday a year, while his dad only had two weeks.

His mother answered, "Well, if he's a good vicar, he needs it. If he isn't, the congregation needs it."

Four businessmen, pillars of their local church, were chatting after dinner one evening. The conversation turned to the subject of honesty, and each agreed in turn to reveal their secret weaknesses to one another.

First: "When I am away from home I sometimes visit dubious nightclubs."

Second: "Although people think I am teetotal I sometimes have a drink on the sly."

Third: "No one knows, but I have a real gambling problem. I can't keep away from the betting shop."

Fourth: "You're not going to like this. I'm a dreadful gossip."

"Father," asked the village reprobate, "What would be this sciatica that I read about?"

The parish priest saw his chance. "Ah," he replied, "You may well ask. A most painful and incurable infliction, and it comes of loose living and bad ways. Those get sciatica who neglect their religious duties, and go after the drink, and lead lives of dissipation."

"I am very grateful to you, Father," the reprobate replied, "and I am glad to know about the sciatica, for I have just read how his Lordship the Bishop is suffering from a severe attack of it."

The Tablet

A rector was visiting his local medical centre when a nun came rushing out, screaming. When he went in to see his doctor, he asked, "As I was coming in I met a nun running away in great distress. Is she all right?"

"Oh, yes," smiled the doctor. "I've just told her that she's pregnant."

"And is she?"

"No," replied the doctor, "but it's cured her hiccups."

One Sunday after the morning service the vicar asked his verger, "Should I put more fire into my sermons?"

The verger replied, "In my opinion, vicar, you should put more sermons into your fire."

The minister's young son wrote to his aunt to apologize for forgetting her birthday. "I'm ever so sorry," he wrote. "I have no excuse, and it would serve me right if you forgot mine, which is next Tuesday."

A clergyman on holiday called at a farm and asked for a drink. He was given a bowl of milk. He noticed a pig watching very intently and remarked that it must be a very intelligent animal.

"Do you think he knows I'm a stranger?" he asked.

"No, reverend," said the farmer, "but he knows that you're using his bowl."

The verger was conducting the vicar to the pulpit for his first sermon in the parish. He whispered, "Vicar, I ought to tell you that there is no record of any soul being saved in this church with a sermon that lasts longer than ten minutes."

A poster advertised a forthcoming discussion at a Ladies' Meeting on the subject "What Makes a Happy Marriage?". One line read,

"WHAT DO YOU AND YOUR HUSBAND HAVE IN COMMON?"

Someone had written below:

WE WERE BOTH MARRIED ON THE SAME DAY.

A CHOICE OF PRAYERS:

Church of England

"O Lord, grant that we may not be like porridge
— stiff, stodgy and hard to stir; but like
cornflakes — crisp, fresh and ready to serve."

Church of Scotland

"O Lord, grant that we may not be like cornflakes — lightweight, empty and cold; but like porridge — warm, comforting and full of natural goodness."

In our small village the vicar has asked us to raise funds for repairs to the church, a new church hall, new hymn books, a new church minibus, and much else.

We are now known not as "the flock" but "the fleeced".

Each year we have a missionary weekend.

Last year, on the preceding Sunday the vicar asked if anyone would like to have the visiting missionary for lunch.

Some years ago I used to play the organ at our local crematorium. One cold frosty morning when the ice made walking difficult, I was plodding through the grounds when a lady observed, "You would think that they would spread some ashes around here, wouldn't you?"

The organist at another crematorium told me that he had to play for the service of a deceased man who weighed 28 stone (nearly 400 pounds).

The opening hymn was "How Great Thou Art".

The heating in our church was from infra-red heaters, and there were the usual complaints of hot heads and cold feet. During the notices I came across a leaflet in my choir stall from the makers, which stated that the effect was intended to be similar to the sun's rays.

The next hymn included: "Sunbeams scorching all the day".

On one occasion at the midweek meeting I spoke on "Heaven and Hell".

At the end of the talk the secretary stood up to give the notices, saying, "Well, friends, it'll soon be time to think about the outing — which place do you want to go to?"

A minister arrived at his new church and was interviewed by a young reporter from the local paper. The minister was in good form and told the reporter many of his finest and funniest stories. "But don't print them," he added. "I want to use them in my sermons."

The frustrated reporter reluctantly agreed, but the minister was horrified to read in the paper the following evening: "The minister told some good stories which cannot be repeated."

A minister on holiday was reading his hometown newspaper and was stunned to read his own obituary.

Shocked and upset, he telephoned the editor to remonstrate.

"Just a minute," came the cautious reply. "Where are you calling from?"

When parishioners of Burton Latimer
used to complain about the cold church,
the rector used to remind them sternly:
"Many are cold but few are frozen."

As a part-time hospital chaplain I was visiting the wards when I encountered a patient from Afghanistan, the top half of whose body was held firmly in a brace. He had never seen a Christian minister before, and noticing my dog collar asked, "What's wrong with your neck?"

Two new loudspeakers will be dedicated at this evening's service. They are a gift from the verger in memory of his wife.

The minister wondered what he could buy his wife for a Golden Wedding present. He saw some attractive musical boxes in a shop window and decided to get her one of these. However, being rather forgetful, he completely forgot to ask if he could hear the tune played. Imagine his wife's surprise when she wound up her gift, only to hear it play,

"The Old Grey Mare, she ain't what she used to be."

The late Archbishop of Canterbury, Lord Runcie, had a great sense of humour. He would undoubtedly have appreciated a report of his funeral in a national newspaper, which added, "His mother was a hairdresser and his roots were very important to him."

From an Oxfordshire parish magazine:

"We are grateful to Mrs Clark for helping the Cub Scouts with their First Aid Tests. We hope she will soon be able to leave hospital."

Visitors are invited to join us in the hall after this service for a cup of coffee. Squash will be available if coffee is not your cup of tea.

72

The preacher for next Sunday will be found hanging on the notice board in the porch.

A minister was visiting a small chapel which could no longer afford to offer the customary travelling expenses to preachers. Instead the steward asked the visitor to accept the sum total of the offertory in lieu.

After the service the steward emptied the offertory bag onto a table and one solitary coin rolled out.

"Here are your expenses," said the steward.

"Is that all there was in the offering?" asked the minister in dismay. "You have only given me back the money I put in myself."

"Well," said the steward, "if you had put more in, you would have got more out."

Chuchyard maintenance is becoming increasingly difficult and it will be appreciated if parishioners will cut the grass around their own graves.

From Kings Lynn Parish Magazine:

**Burial charges are to go up
at the cemetery.
The increased cost of living
is blamed.**

A lady left a note in her will that she should be cremated — and her ashes scattered over Harrods to ensure that her daughter visited her at least twice a week.

A three-year-old boy had been told that God had given mummy a new baby and she was keeping it under her heart until it was big enough to be born.

In the way that only children

can, he chose a moment of silent prayer in the morning service to announce in his loudest voice, "God sent mummy a baby but she's keeping it under her HAT until it's bigger."

Parishioner to vicar's wife: "Did you wake up grumpy this morning?"

Vicar's wife: "No, I thought I'd let him sleep."

The rector was old and very devout, but sometimes far away during the service.

One Sunday during Evensong, as we reached the creed, there was silence, so the curate went across to him, touched his arm gently, and whispered, "I believe in God, sir."

"So do I," replied the rector happily, "so do I."

There will be a procession next Sunday afternoon in the grounds of the monastery. If it should rain in the afternoon the procession will take place on Sunday morning.

An Anglican Archbishop and a Roman Catholic Archbishop both died. When they reached the Pearly Gates, St Peter ushered them into a waiting room. After they had been kicking their heels for an hour or so, a pretty girl arrived and was shown straight in. At this their Graces protested, asking why such a youngster should get preferential treatment over men of their standing.

St Peter looked at them a moment and said: "That young girl has just crashed her sports car which she learned to drive a year ago. In that short year she has put the fear of God into more people than your Graces have in the whole of your lives."

Graveyard rhymes from Dr David Owen:

Here lies Solomon Peas
Under the trees and sod
But Peas is not here —
Only the pod —
Peas is shelled out and gone to God.

Here lies the body of Mary Jones
Who died of eating cherry stones.
Her name was Smith, it was not Jones
But Jones was put to rhyme with stones.

A vicar grew exasperated by the number of people knocking on his door and asking for food, money and clothing. One morning he looked out of his window and saw an old tramp on his knees eating the grass on the front lawn.

"My good man," he cried, "Whatever are you doing there?"

"Well, sir," the tramp replied, "I'm so hungry that I'm eating the grass."

"Then go into the back garden," said the weary vicar. "You'll find it's longer there."

A south London clergyman appointed to another parish received a letter from a firm of furniture removers. It stated, "In the last year we have removed forty south London clergymen to the entire satisfaction of all concerned."

When my nephew was married all went well until he knelt at the altar. Then everyone could see that some wicked individual had written on the sole of his left shoe "HELP" and on the sole of his right shoe "ME".

A missionary deep in the jungle came across a witch doctor pounding his drum furiously.

"What's the matter?" asked the missionary with some trepidation.

"We have no water," responded the witch doctor, drumming away.

"Oh, I see," said the missionary, seeing an opportunity. "You're praying for rain?"

"No, I'm not," replied the witch doctor curtly. "I'm sending for the plumber."

One morning a young lady slipped and was saved by falling heavily into a passing priest. Setting her back on her feet he commented, "This is the first time I've had a fallen woman in my arms."

She replied, "And this is the first time I've been picked up by a priest."

In Louisiana there had been a long drought. A clergyman called a meeting in church to pray for rain, and most of his congregation crowded in.

The clergyman stepped forward and looked sadly around. After some seconds he said,

"The lack of faith in this congregation is a sin and a shame. I fear for your souls. Here we are come together to pray for rain — and not a single one of you has had enough faith to bring an umbrella with you."